The I AM statements of Jesus

By W M Henry

ISBN: 978-1-78364-535-0

www.obt.org.uk

****

The Open Bible Trust
Fordland Mount, Upper Basildon,
Reading, RG8 8LU, UK.

The I AM statements of Jesus

Contents

Page

Study 1
Ego Eimi
and
its meaning

Study 1
Ego Eimi and
its meaning

One popular aspect of Jesus' teaching is His description of Himself using the formula "I am…" Important lessons have been learned from studying the ways in which He is the light of the world, the good shepherd and so on. But what exactly did Jesus mean by the phrase "I am"? The words in Greek are *ego eimi* and when we examine the way Jesus uses this phrase, we discover that He is doing much more than making descriptive statements about Himself.

These studies explore how Jesus uses the expression *ego eimi* in John's Gospel and consider something of what it means.

"Before Abraham was, I am"

In John chapter 8:56, in discussion with the Jews, the Lord pointed out that Abraham rejoiced that he would see His day. This is an ambiguous statement and does more than suggest that Abraham anticipated Jesus' coming. Welch points out that to "see his day" meant that they had fellowship together. If we look at the Jews' reaction, it is clear that this is how they interpreted Jesus' words:

> "You are not yet fifty years old, and have you seen Abraham?" (John 8:57)

It was completely incomprehensible for this young man, the village carpenter, to claim to have interacted with Abraham, but Jesus' reply infuriated the Jews even more:

> Jesus said to them, "Truly, truly I say to you, before Abraham was, I am. (*ego eimi*)" So they picked up stones to throw at him. (John 8:58-59)

Why had His words provoked such an extreme reaction? The answer lies in the fact that, by using the expression *ego eimi,* Jesus was deliberately taking upon Himself the language of deity. When the Lord spoke to Moses from the burning bush, He commissioned him to free the Israelites from slavery in Egypt. Moses asked God to tell him His name. God replied:

> "I AM WHO I AM." And he said, "Say this to the people of Israel, 'I AM has sent me to you.'" (Exodus 3:14)

The Septuagint (the Greek translation of the Old Testament), translates "I AM WHO I AM " as "ego eimi Ho on." So Jesus, by the use of *ego eimi*, was identifying Himself with the God of Israel, who entered into covenant relationship with that nation, delivered them and guided them through their tortuous history.

The Jews recognised what He was saying and regarded such a claim as blasphemous, which was why they wanted to stone Him.

"I AM" – a reflection of uniqueness

The phrase *ego eimi* is an emphatic statement drawing attention to the identity of the speaker. It can be used in everyday speech but only very rarely occurs in the New Testament. In John 9, after Jesus healed the man born blind, the Jews debated as to whether he was the same man, or just someone who looked like him. The man declared:

"I am (*ego eimi*) the man." (John 9:9)

When spoken by God, the name stresses His uniqueness and declares that there is no one like Him. He is superior to all others. It is a declaration of absolute monotheism. "I am and there is no one else!" For anyone else to use this title would be blasphemous in the extreme. So the Jews understood what Jesus was claiming for Himself. It is very difficult for us to grasp how this could be but Jesus is the Word, the One who was with God and who was God in the beginning (John 1:1).

Elsewhere in John's Gospel Jesus claimed that there is an identification between Himself and God the Father. For example He told the Jews that:

"I and the Father are one." (John 10:30)

This claim also prompted the Jews to pick up stones to stone Him, as they had done in chapter 8. Later, when speaking to the disciples, Jesus responded to a question from Philip by saying:

"Whoever has seen me has seen the Father." (John 14:9)

"I AM" – a reflection of timelessness

The name "I AM" also has implications in relation to time. It suggests a permanent existence, which transcends time. He is always the self-existent One, the first and the last, "who is and who was and who is to come" (Revelation 1:8). Sanders & Mastin suggest that although *ego eimi* can be translated as a simple present tense "I am," it also could have a backward-looking view of "I have been and still am." When God spoke to Moses from the bush, He also stated:

> "I am (*ego eimi*) the God of your father, the God of Abraham, the God of Isaac, and the God of Jacob." (Exodus 3:6)

God's connection with this people dated further back than the time of Moses. He was the One who had called Abram in Ur of the Chaldees (Genesis 12:1).

Bullinger, on the other hand, emphasises the future perspective, and, in a footnote to Exodus 3:14 renders the name of God as "I will be what I will be (or become.)"

Jesus' statement about Himself contrasts with what He said about Abraham. Abraham "was" (i.e. "came into being") whereas Jesus "is." He claims to possess the divine life in Himself – a life that is self-sustaining and transcends time. No wonder the Jews were scandalised!

The Lord Jesus stands above and beyond time. He is the Word. In Him the whole fullness of deity dwells bodily (Colossians 2:9).

> "I am the Alpha and the Omega," says the Lord God, "who is and who was and who is to come, the Almighty." (Revelation 1:8)

At the close of the book of Revelation, the glorified Lord Jesus states:

> "I am the Alpha and the Omega, the first and the last, the beginning and the end." (Revelation 22:13)

He was there, in the beginning, and He will be there at the end because He is alive forevermore (Revelation 1:18).

The Lord Jesus, then, came to the people of Israel and identified Himself with the God of their fathers, who stood in covenant relationship with them, the supreme God, who had spoken to Abram, to Isaac, to Jacob and to Moses.

But the Lord also uses the term *ego eimi* in other, less obvious ways in the Gospel of John. And these instances resonate with statements made by the God of Israel about Himself in the prophecy of Isaiah. This will be the subject of the next study.

Study 2
"I AM"
as part of
Jesus' Identity

Study 2

"I AM" as part of Jesus' Identity

The opening study considered the meaning of the Greek words *ego eimi* and the way Jesus used them to identify Himself with the God who revealed Himself to Moses in Exodus 3:14 in the context of His deliverance of Israel from Egypt.

"I am He"

However, this is not the only place in the Old Testament where God claims *ego eimi*. In Isaiah chapters 40-55 God reveals Himself once more as the Deliverer of the nation of Israel. This time their deliverance is not from slavery in Egypt, but from exile in Babylon. In these chapters, Isaiah introduces the "suffering servant" (the Lord Jesus), the Messiah who will redeem and restore His people and ultimately bring justice to the earth. And repeatedly God emphasises His own uniqueness and supremacy with an *ego eimi* statement, regularly translated as "I am he."

For example:

> "Who has performed and done this, calling the generations from the beginning? I, the Lord, the first, and with the last; *I am he*." (Isaiah 41:4)

"You are my witnesses," declares the Lord, "and my servant whom I have chosen, that you may know and believe me and understand that *I am he*." (Isaiah 43:10)

"I, *I am he* who blots out your transgressions for my own sake, and I will not remember your sins." (Isaiah 43:25)

"Listen to me, O Jacob, and Israel, whom I called! *I am he*; I am the first, and I am the last. My hand laid the foundation of the earth, and my right hand spread out the heavens." (Isaiah 48:12-13)

These verses (among others) show God in relation to His people, but much of what He says here is accomplished by the Lord Jesus. He is the Creator of all (John 1:3); He is the first and the last (Revelation 1:17-18); He is the means by which His people's transgressions will be blotted out (Isaiah 53; Acts 8:32-35).

And in John's Gospel, the Lord Jesus, in several places, applies the *ego eimi* title to Himself in such a way as to be rendered "I am He" and the ESV translation reflects this.

The first occurrence is in John 4, where the Lord speaks with a Samaritan woman at a well. He was explaining the nature of true worship to the woman and she responded by saying:

"I know that Messiah is coming (he who is called Christ). When he comes, he will tell us all things." Jesus said to her, "I who speak to you *am he" (ego eimi)*. (John 4:25-26)

There are two other passages where Jesus also claims "I am He." These are in the context of warning the Jews of the consequences of rejecting Him and are both found in John 8, in verses 24 and 28:

> "I told you that you would die in your sins, for unless you believe that *I am he*, you will die in your sins." (verse 24)

> "When you have lifted up the Son of Man, then you will know that *I am he*, and that I do nothing on my own authority, but speak just as the Father taught me." (verse 28)

So Jesus is using God's repeated self-description from Isaiah "I am He," to reveal Himself as the Messiah, the One promised to Israel through Isaiah centuries before. In doing so, He takes on the language of God, linking Himself with the God of Israel.

The Lord's reception by the Jews was very different from His reception by the Samaritan woman. As John said in his opening chapter:

> He came to his own, and his own people did not receive him. But to all who did receive him, who believed on his name, he gave the right to become children of God. (John 1:11-12)

The Jews, who should have recognised Him, largely failed to do so, while the outcast Samaritan hailed Him as "the Christ."

However, there are two other, less obvious passages in which Jesus says *ego eimi* as a means of identifying Himself.

Jesus walking on the water (John 6:16-21)

After the sign of the feeding of the 5,000 the people wanted to make Him king by force and, realising this, Jesus retreated into the mountains by Himself. The disciples, left alone by the lake shore, decided to row across to Capernaum. They soon found themselves facing a strong headwind and, as they struggled to make progress in the dark, they saw the figure of Jesus walking towards them on the water. Unsurprisingly, they were terrified, but He reassured them with the words:

"It is I (*ego eimi*); do not be afraid." (John 6:20)

At first glance this does not appear to be particularly significant. All He was doing was identifying Himself ("Don't worry; it's only me!"). But in the context, as He showed His authority over nature by walking across a lake, He was demonstrating to the disciples that their security lay in the fact that "I am."

Jesus' arrest in Gethsemane (John 18:1-11)

When Jesus was in the Garden of Gethsemane with the 11 disciples, a band of soldiers and officers, led by Judas, came from the chief priests to arrest Him. Their interaction with Him was quite amazing:

Jesus… came forward and said to them, "Whom do you seek?" They answered him, "Jesus of Nazareth." Jesus said to them, "I am he (*ego eimi*)"… When Jesus said to them "I am he" they drew back and fell to the ground. (John 18:4-6)

This is an extraordinary reaction from a group of soldiers faced with an unarmed man, whom they were trying to arrest. And, as in the incident of walking on the water, at one level Jesus is doing nothing more than identifying Himself. Yet the tremendous power in the words *ego eimi* coming from His lips shows that there is something much deeper going on.

In John's Gospel, then, Jesus makes "I am" statements to the nation of Israel as part of His identity as the One who had delivered them in the past and was in covenant relationship with them. He came to reveal the Father and such was their unity that He could say that anyone who had seen Him had seen the Father (John 14:9).

But Jesus also used the expression *ego eimi* to describe certain aspects of His nature and function. These first two studies have considered *ego eimi* as a description of *who* He is; the following chapters will explore *ego eimi* as a description of *what* He is.

Study 3
"I AM
the Bread of
Life"
(John 6:25-59)

Study 3

"I AM the Bread of Life"

(John 6:25-59)

In the Gospels Jesus uses *ego eimi* to introduce various aspects of His function in relation to His Father and to believers. The remaining studies will focus on the famous "I AM" discourses, which provide vivid metaphors to help us to understand the relationship between ourselves, the Lord Jesus and the Father. First, we will explore Jesus' description of Himself as the Bread of Life.

The setting of the discourse

On the day after the Lord fed 5,000 people, the crowd followed Him across the lake to Capernaum. They did this, not because they wanted some spiritual benefit but because He had given them bread, as Jesus drily observed (verse 26).

However, He was offering them much more than a free meal and immediately He turned their attention to "food that endures to eternal life" (verse 27).

There then follows a discussion between Jesus and "the Jews," which took place in the synagogue at Capernaum (verse 59), in which Jesus declares that He is "the Bread of Life" (verses 35, 48 and 51) and that if they eat this bread, they will have eternal life (verse 54).

The outrage of the Jews

The Jews were scandalised at His words, for two reasons: firstly, this was Jesus, the village carpenter, Joseph's boy (verse 42). How could He talk about "coming down from heaven"? Secondly, His words disgusted them. They had carefully observed the dietary requirements of the Law all their lives, so the idea of eating His flesh and drinking His blood (verses 54-56) was simply revolting to them. In fact, verses 60 and 66 tell us that some of His followers found these sayings so difficult that they turned away from Him.

Bread from heaven?

The Jews, as they frequently did, demanded a miraculous sign (verse 30). Their ancestors ate "bread from heaven" in the wilderness. Jesus had just fed 5,000 people with a few loaves and fish on a one-off basis. They had eaten manna for 40 years during their wanderings. Could He replicate that?

Jesus corrected their misunderstanding. First of all, the bread provided by Moses was not the "true bread from heaven" (verse 32); the true bread was the One given by the Father. The focus shifts from what Moses did then to what the Father was doing now; from literal, perishable bread to the Living One who was standing in their presence.

The manna provided through Moses satisfied the Israelites for one day only. They had to go out again the next morning for more. And it did not preserve their lives indefinitely (verse 48).

By contrast:

"I am the living bread that came down from heaven. If anyone eats of this bread, he will live for ever. And the bread that I will give for the life of the world is my flesh… This is the bread that came down from heaven, not like the bread the fathers ate and died. Whoever feeds on this bread will live forever." (verses 51, 58)

Eating the flesh of the Lord Jesus brings eternal life. There in verse 51 the Lord refers to His coming death – the sacrifice for sins that would enable men and women to be forgiven and brought into a relationship with the Lord Jesus and His Father that will continue for eternity.

But how do we eat His flesh and drink His blood?

Eating is believing

In this passage the Lord makes two parallel statements that bring out this truth:

"Truly, truly I say to you, whoever believes has eternal life." (verse 47)

"If anyone eats of this bread, he will live forever." (verse 51)

So, "eating" is equated with "believing". Similarly in verse 35 Jesus, using the poetic technique of repeating thoughts declares:

"I am the bread of life; whoever comes to me shall not hunger, and whoever believes in me shall never thirst."

Again, partaking of this bread is compared to believing.

Similarly, in verse 56, Jesus states that anyone eating His flesh and drinking His blood "abides" in Him, which anticipates His teaching in John 15 that the key to "abiding" in Him is faith and obedience – see, for example, John 15:9-10.

So the Lord, by this powerful metaphor, urges us to believe in Him and enter into a relationship with Him that is so intimate that it can be compared to taking Him into us and making Him a part of us. As He says in His prayer in John 17:

> "I made known to them (the disciples) your name... that the love with which you have loved me may be in them and *I in them*." (John 17:26)

In that prayer the Lord links the disciples with the Father, and in John 6 too He discusses the role of the Father in this work.

The role of the Father

In John 6:57, Jesus explains that "eating" Him brings us life through Him and this process corresponds to the Lord's own relationship with His Father:

> "As the living Father sent me, and I live because of the Father, so whoever feeds on me, he also will live because of me."

Throughout this discourse, the Lord traces the role of the Father in the process of salvation.

The Lord was sent by the Father:
God the Father set His seal of approval on the Son (verse 27) and sent Him, as the Bread of Life, into the world (verses 29, 32, 57).

The process of salvation was initiated by the Father; the Son came to implement His plan.

The Father draws believers to the Son:
In verse 37 Jesus explains that believers are "given" by the Father to the Son. In fact, none of us can come to Jesus unless the Father draw us to Him (verse 44). This truth in no way limits our requirement to respond to the Gospel – our "work" is to believe (verse 29) - but it shows the strong initiative taken by the Father.

Jesus came to do the will of the Father:
Throughout His ministry the Lord Jesus taught that He had not come to do His own will, but the will of the Father (e.g. John 4:34; 5:30). Here in John 6:38, this is explicitly stated again. All that the Lord Jesus did, even His death on the cross, was in obedience to His Father. But in John 6:39-40 Jesus focuses on one particular aspect of the Father's will.

The Father's will is that everyone who believes, will have eternal life:
In verses 39-40, we find a double statement of the Father's will. Firstly, in verse 39, none of those who have been drawn to the Son by the Father will be lost, supplementing Jesus' earlier declaration in verse 37 that He will not turn away anyone who comes to Him. Secondly, in verse 40, all who believe will have eternal life. These two parallel statements are linked by the Lord's repeated promise that He will "raise him up on the last day".

This promise occurs four times in this passage, in verses 39 and 40 (in connection with the Father's will), in verse 44 (in relation to the Father drawing men and women to the Son) and in verse 54 (in connection with the need to "eat" His flesh.) It is expressed as a triumphant refrain, re-enforcing the message that the Lord is giving to us. He was sent into the world by the Father, who draws people to Him. Those who come to Him and commit themselves to Him in faith are brought into a love relationship with the Father and the Son that cannot be broken and that will continue into eternity.

Study 4
"I AM
the Light of the
World"
(John 8:12, 9:5)

Study 4
"I AM the Light of the World"
(John 8:12, 9:5)

During the Feast of Tabernacles, the city of Jerusalem was flooded with the light from four massive lamps, to remind the people of the pillar of fire, which had guided the Israelites in the desert. It was against this background that Jesus made His first declaration in John 8:12 that He was the light of the world and connected that light with life.

> "*I am the light of the world.* Whoever follows me will not walk in darkness but will have the light of life."

In the next chapter, as He prepared to engage with the man born blind, He repeated His statement in verse 5, adding that it was while He was in the world, that He was its light.

> "As long as I am in the world, *I am the light of the world.*" (John 9:5)

The setting for the statement

John 8 records the debate between Jesus and the Jews about the validity of His testimony, about His identity and about His authority. And, although many believed in Him (verse 30), the vast majority did not accept His testimony (verse 13), know His

Father (verse 19), or understand what He was talking about (verse 27). Even those who did believe in Him challenged His teaching that they needed the liberation only He could bring. They claimed that they were already free because they were children of Abraham, only for Jesus to retort that they were, in fact, children of the devil (verse 44). The light had come among them but they could not see it, or allow it to illuminate their surroundings.

In chapter 9, in contrast, we find the man born blind, who was brought into the light in more ways than one. For the first time in his life, he was able to see, but he also came to recognise that his healer was no ordinary teacher, but One who was worthy of worship (verse 38). The Pharisees, on the other hand, remained blind, but because they claimed they could see, they were pronounced guilty (verse 41).

Light and Life

John introduces Jesus as light very early in the Gospel. In the opening chapter we find an echo of the statements made by the Lord in chapters 8 and 9 linking light with life and with His presence in the world:

> In him was life, and the life was the light of men. The light shines in the darkness, and the darkness has not overcome it… The true light which gives light to everyone, was coming into the world (John 1:4-5, 9)

In saying "in him was life" John was meaning much more than "he was alive." The life the Lord possessed was the self-sustaining life that was a characteristic of God, which Jesus identifies as "life in himself."

"For as the Father has life in himself, so he has granted the Son to have life in himself." (John 5:26)

But Jesus, like the Father, has the ability to pass resurrection life on to men and women:

"For, as the Father raises the dead and gives them life, so also the Son gives life to whom he will." (John 5:21)

We will never possess "life in ourselves;" we do not become God, as we will always look to Him as the Giver of life. He has come so that we might have life to the full (John 10:10) and if we hear His word and believe in the One who sent Him we have "passed from death to life" (John 5:24). So Jesus brings light in the sense of bringing life.

Light and Truth

Light is also connected with truth. Evildoers avoid light because it would reveal their wrongdoing, but:
> ... whoever does what is true comes to the light, so that it may be clearly seen that his works have been carried out in God. (John 3:21)

Light has the sense of knowledge and understanding; light reveals what is going on in the darkness. Jesus was declaring Himself to be the light of the world but the Jewish leaders would have none of it, bickering with Him, challenging His authority and refusing to come to Him or His Father.

The incident of the man born blind in chapter 9 is a case study of an apparently unlikely person being transformed by coming to see the truth in Jesus. The change is so great that his friends and neighbours doubted that he was the same man (verses 8-9). As we read the incident, we see his growing courage in challenging the Pharisees about the inconsistency of their arguments, even as his frightened parents tried to distance themselves from him (verses 20-22). Eventually he was insulted by the Pharisees and thrown out of the synagogue (verse 34).

We can also see his developing understanding that Jesus was "a prophet" (verse 17), "a man from God" (verse 33), to the point where he worshiped Him as "Son of Man" (verse 38). It is important to remember that no Jew would ever worship a man. Only God was to be worshiped. The fact that he offered worship to Jesus showed that he recognised that He was the Christ. He had come to the light, and he was never the same again.

Light and Darkness

The coming of the Lord Jesus into the world was the watershed of history. God's light had shone into the world's darkness and Jesus came to call His people "out of darkness and into his marvellous light" (1 Peter 2:9). As Jesus says in John 12:46:

> "I have come into the world as light, so that whoever believes in me may not remain in darkness."

In the same chapter Jesus warns the Jews that the light would only be with them for a little while longer so:

> "While you have the light, believe in the light, that you may become sons of light." (John 12:36)

Unfortunately, many people will not come to the Light, or believe in Him, preferring to remain in the darkness of ignorance and error. As Jesus Himself sadly observed:

> "This is the judgment: the light has come into the world, and people loved the darkness rather than the light, because their works were evil." (John 3:19)

"This is the judgment" - the coming of the Lord Jesus inevitably brings judgment. As He told the Pharisees after healing the blind man:

> "For judgment I came into this world, that those who do not see may see, and those who see may become blind." (John 9:39)

We all have a choice to make – either we come to the Light, taking that Light into ourselves by faith and so become "sons of light," or we continue to live in darkness. Western society has largely rejected its Christian heritage and turned away from the truth. As a consequence we are living in an environment of relativism, post truth and fake news. We find confusion and uncertainty in the arena of politics, in morality and in finding values to live by. Having rejected the Lord, the true Light, people have no reference point outside themselves and are completely in the dark. As Jesus said in the Sermon on the Mount:

> "If then the light in you is darkness, how great is the darkness!" (Matthew 6:23)

But still the Light shines, no longer a physical presence among us but coming to us through the Scriptures, through prayer and through the power of His Spirit. If we follow Him we will become children of Light, and He will shine on our path giving us purpose and values that have implications for eternity. Paul, writing to the Ephesian Christians, tells them:

> Walk as children of light (for the fruit of the light is found in all that is good and right and true), and try to discern what is pleasing to the Lord. (Ephesians 5:8-10)

If we can make that our basis for living, we will be true children of our Father.

Study 5
"I AM
the Door
of the Sheep"
(John 10:1-10)

Study 5

"I AM the Door of the Sheep"
(John 10:1-10)

In the first part of John 10, the Lord uses a complex metaphor about sheep and shepherding, culminating in His famous declaration in verses 11-18 that He is the Good Shepherd, who lays down His life for His sheep. However, in the first ten verses a different picture emerges. Twice (in verses 7 and 9), He states that He is "the door" to the sheepfold. Some commentators have argued that this is merely an extension of His role as the Good Shepherd, conjuring up the image of the shepherd lying down at night in the open doorway of the sheep pen so that nothing can come in or out without his knowledge. However, there are separate issues that need to be considered, so it is worth exploring this image separately.

The setting for the statement

In the opening five verses of the chapter Jesus sets the scene and introduces several characters to us. We have the sheepfold – an open, walled area with one door. This door is guarded by a gatekeeper (verse 3), who only opens it to shepherds whom he recognises. This security is important because there are thieves and robbers about (verse 1). There may be several flocks of sheep within the pen but each sheep knows the voice of its shepherd and will follow him only (verses 3-4). They will not follow a stranger because they do not know him (verse 5).

It is all rather confusing since up to this point, the Lord has not explained who any of these characters represent. It is therefore not surprising to find in verse 6 that His audience did not understand what He was saying to them.

So from verse 7 onwards He starts to unpack His message and explain His figure of speech to them. He begins by declaring:

> "Truly, truly I say to you, 'I am the door of the sheep.'"

As frequently happens in John's Gospel, when the Lord explains a statement His hearers have found confusing, the explanation initially seems to complicate things further rather than clarify the matter. So in this case; if He is the door (and the shepherd), then who is the gatekeeper and how does he open the door in response to the shepherd's voice? And what does the sheepfold represent? It is probably best not to allegorise Jesus' figures of speech as there are some characters, like the gatekeeper and the stranger, who cannot really be matched with particular real life characters. Instead we should focus on the main points that He is trying to make and ignore the peripheral aspects of the story.

In verse 9, Jesus repeats His statement but supplements it with an explanation:

> "I am the door. If anyone enters by me, he will be saved and will go in and out and find pasture."

So what does Jesus mean by declaring Himself to be the door to the sheep pen? There are two main truths He is trying to put across:

He is the only means of access to the sheep pen

There is only one door to the pen. Anyone who tries to get in by another way, climbing over the wall, is a thief and a robber (verse 1). If the sheep are the Lord's people and the pen is the place where they find salvation and protection, then the Lord, as the only means of access to that place, is claiming His *exclusivity* here. He is *the* door in the same sense in which He is *the* Way. As He said plainly to the disciples in John 14:6:

> "No one comes to the Father except through me."

It is important that we don't downplay what Jesus is saying here. Jesus is the only way to the Father. This has always been the message of the Gospel. When Peter and John faced the Jewish Council, Peter, speaking in the power of the Holy Spirit, told them that:

> "There is salvation in no one else, for there is no other name under heaven given among men, by which we must be saved." (Acts 4:12)

In our relativistic world this message is not popular but it remains true. If we could reach God by some other way there would have been no need for Jesus to die for us. But God's love for us is so profound that He was prepared to send His Son to pay the ultimate price for our sin, so that we might be free. The Gospel is not one option among many. It is *the* power of God for salvation to everyone who believes (Romans 1:16).

In verse 8 the Lord states that all who came before Him were thieves and robbers, suggesting false Messiahs like Theudas and Judas, who are referred to in Acts 5:36-37. Jesus' use of the word "came" indicates that they claimed to be someone special and drew the people to them, only for it all to end in disillusionment. Jesus, on the other hand, was the true and living way to the Father.

But the picture of the Lord Jesus as a secure door has a second message to teach us.

Jesus provides security and protection for His sheep

The door, while providing access, is not designed to keep the sheep permanently inside the pen. That would be no life at all, huddled together, fearful of what was going on outside, but relieved that they have no contact with anything beyond the pen. John 10:9 makes it clear that the sheep go in and out of the door and find pasture.

This picture of the sheep freely moving in and out of the door suggests their complete security and thriving in a life of freedom from fear. Going in and out was an Old Testament expression meaning living a life of peaceful prosperity (e.g. Numbers 27:17). This is what God calls us to. He does not take us out of the world; He wants us to remain in the world and to live life in all its fullness. As He says to the disciples in verse 10

"I came that they may have life and have it abundantly."

While He was with the disciples, Jesus had protected them by His presence. But as He was preparing to leave them He prayed to His Father:

"I do not ask that you take them out of the world, but that you keep them from the evil one." (John 17:15)

The Lord Jesus would no longer be in the world physically but in His place we have the Holy Spirit, who lives within every believer, guiding and protecting us as we live in a hostile environment where there are "thieves and robbers". We do not belong in the world, just as He did not belong here. But as His sheep, He asks us to live counter-culturally, not in an isolated way or a holy huddle within our pen but making a difference as salt and light in the world. Just as the Father sent Him, so He sends us into the world (John 17:18) to bear witness to Him and to introduce those we meet to our Shepherd.

The relationship between the Lord Jesus and His sheep is developed more fully in His discourse on the Good Shepherd, which forms the second part of John 10. This will be the subject of the next chapter.

Study 6
"I AM
the Good
Shepherd"
(John 10:11-18)

Study 6
"I AM the Good Shepherd"
(John 10:11-18)

The picture of the Lord as a shepherd is a recurring idea in the Old Testament – Psalm 23 being the obvious example. Psalm 80 addresses the Lord as "Shepherd of Israel" (verse 1) and exhorts Him to save and restore His people. In Ezekiel 34, the prophet speaks against the leaders of Israel, describing them as shepherds who have fattened themselves rather than the flock and not nurtured and cared for the people. Ezekiel prophesies that the Lord will be their shepherd, seeking out His sheep, rescuing them from the places to which they have been scattered and bringing them into good pasture (verses 11-15).

In John 10:11-18 the Lord echoes Ezekiel's message, declaring that He is the Good Shepherd, in contrast to the hired hand, who cares nothing for the sheep and preserves his own life when the flock is attacked.

The setting for the statement

Jesus has been in an ongoing debate with the Jewish leaders about His identity. Is He the Christ? Has He been sent by God or is He just another charlatan? In John chapter 9 we find Jesus healing the man born blind. His experience is a case study illustrating Ezekiel's message. Israel's "shepherds," the Pharisees are blind guides. They rejected Jesus because He healed on the Sabbath. They threatened and bullied the man rather than caring for him and eventually threw him out of the synagogue (9:34). When Jesus, the Good Shepherd, heard what had happened, He went looking for the man and found him (9:35) revealed His identity to him and accepted his worship (9:35-38).

Jesus states that He is the Good Shepherd in two places in chapter 10, and these relate to the two dimensions of the Good Shepherd's activity:

> "I am the good shepherd. The good shepherd lays down his life for the sheep." (verse 11)

> "I am the good shepherd. I know my own and my own know me." (verse 14)

The Good Shepherd lays down His life for the sheep

In the opening ten verses of the chapter, the Lord declares Himself to be the door of the sheep (see previous chapter). The door is there to provide protection for the sheep from being attacked by thieves and robbers. The Good Shepherd is contrasted, not with thieves and robbers, but with the hired hand, who does not necessarily mean any harm to the flock. However, he is only interested in his own welfare and will desert the sheep when they are attacked by wolves or other predators, because he cares nothing for them (verses 12-13). The Good Shepherd, by contrast, cares for the sheep to the extent of laying down His life for them (verses 11, 15).

We might admire a shepherd with such love for his sheep, but, ultimately, a shepherd dying to protect his sheep is a failure. What good is a dead shepherd to the sheep? But in verses 17-18 the Lord indicates that His death is unique in two ways. Firstly, it is deliberate, in that He lays down His life rather than being killed by His enemies, and secondly, it is temporary, because the Father has given Him the power to take it again:

> "For this reason the Father loves me, because I lay down my life that I may take it up again. No one takes it from me, but I lay it down of my own accord. I have authority to lay it down, and I have authority to take it up again. This charge I have received from my Father." (John 10:17-18)

The Lord's death for His sheep did more than deliver them from their immediate enemies; it gave them eternal life and brought them into relationship with Him and His Father. The involvement of the Father in the process of salvation is explained more fully in the second dimension of the Good Shepherd's work.

The Good Shepherd knows His sheep and is known by them

The picture of the shepherd painted in John 10 brings out the mutual knowledge that exists between a Middle Eastern shepherd and his sheep. As Jesus explains in verses 3-5, the shepherd does not drive the sheep before him into the pasture; he knows each of them by name and calls them individually. They, in turn, recognise his voice and follow him, something they would not do for a stranger.

Unfortunately, as verse 6 tells us, the people did not know what He was talking about. No doubt they knew the practice of shepherds, but what was the point of the story? Jesus explains in the following verses. He is the door of the sheepfold, protecting His sheep from thieves and robbers (verses 7-10), but He is also the Good Shepherd, who cares for His sheep and is trusted by them:

> "I am the good shepherd. I know my own and my own know me, just as the Father knows me and I know the Father." (verses 14-15)

As He does elsewhere in John's Gospel, the Lord Jesus describes the relationship between Him and believers as being parallel to the relationship between His Father and Him (see, e.g. John 15:9; 17:18). It is important to realise that the Father is behind all the Jesus does. The death of the shepherd to save the sheep was part of the Father's plan. He loved the Son for His obedience to death on a cross (verse 17 - see also Philippians 2:8-11) because, as a result of the Shepherd's willingness to sacrifice Himself, the sheep are brought into a flock in which they can know God personally and be known as named individuals, by Him.

But who are the sheep? The immediate flock were the believing ones of Israel, who recognised that the Lord Jesus was their promised Messiah, and put their faith in Him. But God's plan was not limited to a small, geographically localised group.

> "I have other sheep that are not of this fold. I must bring them also and they will listen to my voice. So there will be one flock, one shepherd." (verse 16)

As the book of Acts unfolds, we read of the message being taken to Jewish people scattered throughout the Roman world. Then we find individual Gentiles like Cornelius being filled with the Holy Spirit and brought into God's people. Finally, after the end of Acts we read of a body of believers in which Gentiles are no longer aliens and strangers but:

… fellow heirs, members of the same body, and partakers of the promise in Christ Jesus through the Gospel. (Ephesians 3:6)

"One flock, one shepherd…"

The post-script:
The Lord, His sheep and His Father (verses 22-30)

In verse 19, attention switches to the Jews' response to Jesus' claims and, as usual, there is no agreement. Some think He is demon-possessed, while others argue that no demon could say or do the things He does. Matters come to a head in verse 24 when the Jews confront Him and demand to know whether He is the Christ or not. Jesus' reply pulls together His teaching in this chapter about Himself, His sheep and His Father.

First, He summarises what he has been saying about His role as the Good Shepherd in relation to His sheep.

> "My sheep hear my voice, and I know them, and they follow me. I give them eternal life, and they will never perish, and no one will snatch them out of my hand." (verses 27-28)

His death for the sheep has brought them eternal life. His sheep know Him and follow Him and they are completely secure in His hands. But part of the security that His sheep enjoy comes from the fact that, as well as the shepherd, He is also the door of the sheep. He is the only means of access to a place of blessing and He is the only means of access to the Father (see John 14:6).

And it is the role of the Father that Jesus focuses on in the second part of His summary:

> "My Father, who has given them to me, is greater than all, and no one is able to snatch them out of the Father's hand. I and the Father are one." (verses 29-30)

Again we can see the parallel between the Lord and His Father. In verse 28, His sheep are safe in Jesus' hand; in verse 29, they are in the Father's hand. How can this be? Because He and the Father are one.

Christian believers are gifted eternal life through the death and resurrection of the Son and brought into a loving family relationship, not only with the Son but with the Father also. In fact, the Father is the initiator of the process! At the start of verse 29, Jesus makes the small but significant remark that it is the Father who has given the sheep to the Son.

Later, as the Lord prepared for the ordeal of the cross, He prayed for future believers, that they would be brought into that same one-ness that exists between Himself and the Father:

> "(I ask) that they may all be one , just as you, Father, are in me, and I in you, that they also may be in us, so that the world may believe that you have sent me. The glory that you have given me I have given to them, that they may be one even as we are one, I in them and you in me, that they may become perfectly one, so that the world may know that you sent me and loved them even as you loved me." (John 17:21-23)

The depths of these possibilities are beyond our fathoming, but the security that they offer is total. We are in His and the Father's hands; we are members of His flock knowing Him and being known by Him; we can be one, not just with each other but with Him and the Father.

What a place to be!

Study 7
"I AM
the
Resurrection
and the Life"
(John 11:17-26)

Study 7

"I AM the Resurrection
and the Life"
(John 11:17-26)

The context in which the Lord made His claim to be the Resurrection and the Life was the raising of Lazarus, which is documented in John 11. John's Gospel contains a series of miraculous "signs" performed by Jesus and this miracle was the final sign before the crucifixion. Arguably it anticipates the Lord's own death and resurrection to a greater extent than any other sign recorded by John.

It would appear that the Lord deliberately delayed His visit to Lazarus and his sisters so that Lazarus would be dead before He went to Bethany. In fact, Lazarus had been dead for four days by the time Jesus and His disciples reached the village (verse 39). He was now buried and, humanly speaking, all hope was gone. Although it may seem harsh for Mary and Martha (and for Lazarus too for that matter) to make them go through this experience, the Lord seems to have wanted to crown His healing ministry with a demonstration of His authority over the ultimate enemy, death. By doing this, He would bring glory to both the Father and the Son (John 11:4) by providing proof that He is, indeed, the Resurrection and the Life.

But Lazarus was brought *back* from death to mortal life; he would die again. However, the death and raising of Lazarus prefigured the ultimate triumph of the Lord Jesus who would pass *through* death and out the other side to resurrection life. This would bring even greater glory to God and, indeed, on more than one occasion Jesus referred to His coming passion as His "glorification" (e.g. see John 12:23).

The setting for the statement

The more immediate setting for the Lord's statement was His conversation with Martha, outside the village, prior to the raising of Lazarus. Hearing that the Lord was coming, Martha went out to meet Him and suggested to Him that, if only He had been present, He could have prevented Lazarus from dying (verse 21) – an opinion echoed by Mary in verse 32. It was likely that the sisters, in the terrible days of Lazarus's illness and death, had repeated this thought to one another. If only the Lord were here!

Jesus comforted Martha with the reassurance that Lazarus would rise again. She assumed that He was repeating the orthodox Jewish view that there would be a general resurrection at the last day, a thought which she does not appear to find particularly comforting in her time of grief (verse 24). However, Jesus had something much more radical in mind.

Jesus *is* the Resurrection and the Life

> Jesus said to her, "I am the resurrection and the life. Whoever believes in me, though he die, yet shall he live, and everyone who lives and believes in me shall never die. Do you believe this?" (verses 25-26)

Martha's response to this was to express her faith in Jesus as the Christ (Messiah) and Son of God (verse 27). However, it is still doubtful that she understood Jesus' self-declaration to mean more than a statement that *He* was the One who would raise Lazarus (and everyone else) at the last day. After all, Jesus Himself had claimed this earlier (see John 6:39, 54). But Martha was to see a more immediate demonstration of the Lord's authority. A future dimension of Christian experience was about to materialise in the world. Resurrection was not a vague hope for the future – it was a reality in the present. How could this be? Because of the presence in that small village of the One who is the Resurrection and the Life – the Christ, the Son of God.

John is an extremely skilful writer and, in his reporting of the conversation between the Lord and Martha, he highlights Jesus' identity as Christ and Son of God. It is important to note that the Lord does not say that He *brings* resurrection and life. He *is* Himself the Resurrection and the Life, just as He *is* the Bread of Life and the Light of the World. This great claim resonates with His teaching elsewhere in the Gospel; He possesses life in Himself and has authority to pass that life on to others (John 5:26); in Him was life and that life is the light of men (John 1:4); He came that we may have abundant life (John 10:10).

A double promise

The Lord's *I AM* statement in John 11:25 has two parts to it – "I am the Resurrection" and "I am the Life." This double statement is followed by a double promise:

> "Whoever believes in me, though he die, yet shall he live." (verse 25)

> "Whoever lives and believes in me shall never die." (verse 26)

The first part of the promise corresponds to the Lord's statement that He is the Resurrection. Although physical death is the fate of us all, we can face it in the sure and certain hope of the resurrection, that wonderful day when:

> "... the dead will hear the voice of the Son of God, and those who hear will live." (John 5:25)

The second part of the promise illustrates His claim to be the Life. So it can be understood as following on from the first part; the resurrection life that the dead receive will be eternal. This is certainly true. As Jesus said in John 3:16:

> "For God so loved the world, that he gave his only Son, that whoever believes in him should not perish but have *eternal life*."

Alternatively, in His double promise, the Lord could have been speaking of two different groups of people – those who are alive when He returns (who will never die) and those who have previously died (who will be raised and never die again.) Paul describes what will happen as an encouragement to the Thessalonians:

> For the Lord himself will descend from heaven with a cry of command, with the voice of an archangel, and with the sound of the trumpet of God. And the dead in Christ will rise first. Then we who are alive, who are left, will be caught up together with them in the clouds to meet the Lord in the air, and so we will always be with the Lord. (1 Thessalonians 4:16-17)

As in John 5:25, the voice of the Lord is a key element in the sequence of events. He descends "with a cry of command," the dead are raised and the living are transformed. Of course, Paul was writing at a time when the Lord's return was regarded as imminent, probably during his own lifetime and that of his readers (he describes those living at that time as "we"). Nevertheless, the consummation of the hope of believers throughout history is linked to that great day when the Lord will again step into our world to bring His purposes to a conclusion.

> Our citizenship is in heaven, and from it we await a Saviour, the Lord Jesus Christ, who will transform our lowly body to be like his glorious body, by the power that enables him even to subject all things to himself. (Philippians 3:20-21)

A unique perspective...

Virtually all religions envisage life after death in some form or other. The Christian faith is unique in that it is centred on one individual – the Lord Jesus, the man who is also God. He was there in the beginning of the old creation (John 1:1), the image of the invisible God, the firstborn of all creation (Colossians 1:15), a position of supremacy. Similarly He is supreme over the new creation, the firstborn from the dead (Colossians 1:18), the Resurrection and the Life, pre-eminent in everything (Colossians 1:18).

Study 8
"I AM
the Way,
the Truth and
the Life"
(John 14:1-14)

Study 8
"I AM the Way, the Truth and the Life"
(John 14:1-14)

This "I AM" statement is one of the most difficult to understand. How can someone be the way to the place where they are going, as Jesus appears to be saying in John 14:4-6? No wonder the disciples were baffled and confused.

The context of Jesus' statement was His final teaching to the disciples, in preparation for His departure from them. This teaching was given as He celebrated His final Passover with them and is contained in John 14-17.

Already they were in a state of agitation, following the events of chapter 13. If they had thought that this was going to be just another Passover, they were in for a surprise. First, their Master washed their feet – a shocking thing to do; next He predicted that one of them would betray Him and in the confusion that followed, Judas left. Then He told them that He was about to leave them and that they could not follow Him at this time. Peter, who initially refused to have his feet washed by the Lord, finished the chapter by protesting that he would die for Jesus, only to be told that by the next morning he would have denied three times that he knew Him.

The Setting for the Statement

So, what did Jesus mean by declaring that He was the Way, the Truth and the Life? The immediate setting for His statement was a question from Thomas. Jesus began chapter 14 by attempting to reassure the shocked disciples.

> "Let not your hearts be troubled. Believe in God; believe also in me." (John 14:1)

By this the Lord was asking them to equate their trust in God with their trust in Him – a ridiculously arrogant thing for any normal man to say. This identification of Himself and His Father was central to the meaning of His claim to be the Way, the Truth and the Life. His teaching in the first 14 verses of John 14 is all focussed on the fact that He and the Father are one. The place He was going was His Father's house, so "the way" is the way to the Father. He is the way because He came to reveal the Father and, in effect, brought the Father to us.

Having given this instruction in the opening verse, Jesus then further reassured them that He was going to His Father's house to prepare a place for them and that, when He was ready, He would come and take them there. But His final remark confused them further and prompted Thomas's question.

> "… And you know the way to where I am going." Thomas said to him, "Lord, we do not know where you are going. How can we know the way?" (John 14:4-5)

In his Gospel, John frequently records Jesus using questions arising from His teaching as a basis for providing further information and here He answered Thomas with His great claim:

"I am the way, the truth and the life. No one comes to the Father, except through me." (John 14:6)

The way, *the* truth and *the* life

The first thing that strikes us is the fact that Jesus does not see Himself as one way among many, to the Father; He is *the* way. This is further confirmed by the final comment at the end of verse 6.

In our postmodern society claims like this are scorned as being arrogant or narrow-minded but at the heart of the Christian message is the presentation of the Lord Jesus as God incarnate and this is why He is *the* way. In Him, as Paul says, the whole fullness of deity dwells bodily (Colossians 2:9); He is the visible image of the invisible God (Colossians 1:15); He is Immanuel – God with us (Matthew 1:23). God came down to us in the person of Jesus to enable us to come back to Him. Jesus' identification with His Father is further developed in the following verses.

The Lord's identification with His Father

Immediately, in verse 7, Jesus picked up this theme:

> "If you had known me, you would have known the Father also. From now on you do know him and have seen him."

There is a note of reproof in Jesus comment; if they had really known Him properly, they would have known the Father too. How was this possible? Jesus' baffling final sentence invited a further request, this time from Philip:

"Lord, show us the Father and it is enough for us." (verse 8)

The Lord's response in verses 9-11 highlighted the truth and the extent of His unity with the Father. Anyone who had seen Him, had seen the Father; He is in the Father and the Father is in Him; His words were the Father's words; His works were the Father's works. We sense the Lord's frustration that the disciples had failed to grasp this after three years in His company. To know Him was to know the Father. That is the reason He is *the* way to the Father, rather than *a* way.

The way *and* the truth *and* the life?

But what exactly, does Jesus mean by this triple claim? Is He making three separate statements or saying something else? Some writers have suggested that He is actually making the single statement that He is the way to the Father and that "the truth" and "the life" describe the nature of that way. So, He is really saying something like "I am the true and living way."

This is certainly consistent with the main thrust of the passage which is focussed more on the way, than on truth or life. But when we take on board the fact that Jesus is the Father's self-revelation to us we can see that He *is* truth and He *is* life.

Jesus is truth in two ways: firstly, He is a true revelation of the Father. If we want to know what God is like, we look to Jesus. But secondly, He is truth in a more profound sense in that truth is a fundamental characteristic of God. At the end of his first epistle, John bears witness to Jesus' revelation of the Father

We know that the Son of God has come and has given us understanding, so that we may know him who is true; and we are in him who is true, in his Son Jesus Christ. He is the true God and eternal life. (1 John 5:20)

John sees the Father and the Son as so integrated that it is difficult for us to know which of them John is speaking of in the final sentence of that verse. As he declared at the start of his Gospel, he and his fellow-disciples encountered the Word who was with God in the beginning and who was God (John 1:1).

> And the Word became flesh and dwelt among us, and we have seen his glory, glory as of the only Son from the Father, full of grace and *truth*. (John 1:14)

In what sense is Jesus life? In John 5:26 Jesus makes an extraordinary declaration that:

> "… as the Father has life in himself, so he has granted the Son also to have life in himself."

Jesus, then, possesses the self-sustaining life of God. Not only so, but He has been given authority to pass that life on to men and women.

> "For as the Father raises the dead and gives them life, so also the Son gives life to whom he will." (John 5:21)

The Lord Jesus is the complete revelation of the Father. The God of truth has made Himself known in His Son; the God of life has granted His Son the authority to pass immortal life on to mankind and, as a result, the Son has become the way for the relationship between fallen humanity and the Father not only to be restored, but to be taken to a new level.

Study 9
"I AM
the True Vine"
(John 15:1-17)

Study 9

"I AM the True Vine"

(John 15:1-17)

In the first part of John 15, the Lord explores the relationships between the Father, the Son and the disciples and how these relationships can be maintained. He does this by an allegory depicting Himself as a vine, with the disciples as its branches and the Father as the Gardener, who tends the plant.

The Gardener's work consists of removing branches that are unfruitful and pruning fruitful branches to increase their fruitfulness. The Lord also makes the obvious point that for branches to be fruitful they need to remain attached to the vine, so that the sap from the vine can flow into them and nourish them. If they separate themselves from the vine, they will become useless and fit only to be cut off and burned (verse 6).

But what does this allegory mean? How does the Father "prune" disciples? How do disciples remain connected to the vine that is Christ? And how do they bear fruit? What do these things mean in real terms?

The Setting for the Statement

The Lord's statement that He is the true vine is made during the upper room discourse with His disciples, immediately prior to His arrest and crucifixion. In John 15, He presents, in picture form, some of the truths that He has been explaining in chapter 14 such as the mutual indwelling of the disciples and Himself, which is a function of their love and obedience to Him (14:20-24). Chapter 15 also echoes the previous chapter's comments about answered prayer (14:13-14) and the glory of God (14:13).

In addition, chapter 14 introduces the coming Holy Spirit (14:15-21, 25-26), and, although the first 17 verses of chapter 15 do not mention Him by name, it is He who will be the means of developing fruit in the disciples and in us (see Galatians 5:22-23).

But what, exactly, is Jesus trying to teach by this illustration?

How does the Father "prune" disciples?

The word translated "prune" in verse 2 is related to the word translated "clean" in verse 3.

> "… every branch that does bear fruit he *prunes*, that it may bear more fruit… Already you are *clean* because of the word that I have spoken to you." (verses 2-3)

The disciples had already been cleansed by the truths the Lord had taught them. He had been with them for over three years, teaching them by word and example. They now finally were beginning to get an understanding of who He was, and they were dedicated to Him. Their lives had been transformed. So they were ready to go out and bear fruit.

But in order to do so on an ongoing basis, they required *continually* to abide in the Lord and He in them. The pruning process must continue.

How do disciples abide in Him?

Twice in this passage (verses 4 and 5) the Lord states that the key to bearing fruit is to abide in Him and to allow Him to abide in us. And verse 7 gives us a clue as to what this means:

> "If you abide in me, and *my words* abide in you, ask whatever you wish, and it will be done for you."

In 14:20-24, the Lord said that if the disciples hold His commandments in their hearts and obey them, then He and the Father will love the disciples and come to make their home with them. In 15:9-10 the Lord again speaks of abiding through obedience in the context of love.

> As the Father has loved me, so have I loved you. Abide in my love. If you keep my commandments you will abide in my love, just as I have kept my Father's commandments and abide in His love.

If the disciples love the Lord they will keep His commandments (John 14:15). That is also the message of chapter 15. True love for Jesus causes us to cherish His words and put His commandments into practice. If we do this, we remain in union with Him and He with us.

How do disciples bear fruit?

What does it actually mean to bear fruit? There are a variety of aspects to it, which can all be summed up as the development of a character similar to that of Christ. However, in this passage, the focus is on one particular command – that they should love one another with the same self-sacrificing love that Jesus showed to them.

> "This is my commandment, that you love one another as I have loved you." (verse 12)

This is the love that makes them willing to lay down their lives for their friends (verse 13). This does not necessarily mean literally dying (although it could include that). In his first epistle, John repeats this idea but then immediately sets it in the context of daily living.

> By this we know love, that he laid down his life for us, and we ought to lay down our lives for the brothers. But if anyone has the world's goods and sees his brother in need, yet closes his heart against him, how does God's love abide in him? (1 John 3:16-17)

We lay down our lives for one another by sacrificial giving performed not in one glorious moment of martyrdom, but quietly and continuously in the daily grind of life.

The consequences of obedience

Obedience to the Lord's commands has consequences that affect the Father, the Son and the believer.

The Father is glorified.

In John 15:8, the Lord states that the Father is glorified if disciples bear fruit. John 14:13 indicates that the Father is glorified in the Son, when the Son answers the prayers of disciples, which He promises He will do for those who abide in Him (15:7).

The glorification of the Father is paramount. As Jesus contemplated His imminent ordeal on the cross, His focus was on the glorification of the name of the Father:

> "Now is my soul troubled. And what shall I say? 'Father, save me from this hour?' But for this purpose I have come to this hour. Father, glorify your name." Then a voice came from heaven: "I have glorified it and I will glorify it again." (John 12:27-28)

Similarly for us 2,000 years later, our focus should be on glorifying the Father, by our obedience to the Lord Jesus. It is not for our glory, but for His. However, obedience also has consequences for disciples.

Their relationship with the Lord becomes more intimate.

In John 15:13 the Lord describes the love to which He calls believers as the kind of love that causes them to be prepared to lay down their lives for their friends. But immediately He adds that they are *His* friends if they obey:

> "You are my friends if you do what I command you. No longer do I call you servants…" (John 15:14-15a)

Obedience beings about a transition from servants to friends. What is the difference?

> "… for the servant does not know what his master is doing; but I have called you friends, for all that I have

heard from my Father I have made known to you." (John 15:15b)

What a privilege to be a friend of God and to be taken into His confidence! And the Lord fulfilled that promise by revealing His plans and purposes to the disciples and to subsequent believers through the Spirit-inspired wrings of Luke, Paul and others.

Their prayer requests are answered.

In both chapters 14 and 15 the Lord repeatedly states that either He or the Father will grant "whatever" prayer requests are made by disciples if they abide in Him (see 14:13, 14; 15:7, 16).

So what are we to make of these promises? It is patently not true that every prayer request is granted. Various explanations have been offered as to what Jesus meant – was it a statement limited to the 11 disciples or was it only for a short period of time? Does its fulfilment depend on the strength of faith that believers exercise so that if we have enough faith God will give us anything we ask?

We need to be careful about how we interpret statements including the words like "whatever" as they are not usually as universal in scope as they appear to be. No sensible and loving father would give his son *anything* he asked for and often our prayer requests are inappropriate because of our limited understanding and mixed motives. It is clear from the incident in Acts 12, where James was murdered and Peter arrested by Herod that the disciples' prayers were not all being answered as they would have liked. And when their prayers for Peter's release *were* answered, they were astonished. So there was obviously no expectation that God would give them "anything" they asked.

However, what we can draw from Jesus' promises is that if we will walk in the Lord's ways, abiding in Him and Him in us, He will hear our prayers and answer them according to His wisdom and His purposes. We may not receive "whatever" we ask for but we should be thankful for that.

In conclusion

In this section of John's Gospel the Lord has explained a great deal to the disciples about what He expects from them. He has done this in discussion with them in chapter 14, by the drama of washing their feet in chapter 13 and finally by the allegory of the vine and the branches in chapter 15.

The message is clear: Jesus' followers have been purified by the word He has spoken to them but in order to be people who fulfil their potential in Christ they need to "abide" in Him by allowing His words to be the driving force of their lives. This requires willing obedience, and the particular aspect Jesus focuses on is love for one another. Self-sacrificial love is the very essence of God's people. It is how the world will know that we are His disciples (John 13:35).

We are given the power to do this by Him "abiding" in us, by Him and the Father making their home with us (John 14:23) through the Spirit, who is with us and in us (John 14:17).

Study 10
The Message
of the
Metaphors

Study 10
The Message of the Metaphors

This series of studies has explored the Lord Jesus' use of the phrase *ego eimi* – "I am" to describe Himself and reveal aspects of His character. But what are the common ideas contained in these statements and what are the overall messages conveyed by the different metaphors He uses?

This final chapter will attempt to pull the threads together and summarise the Lord's *ego eimi* teaching about Himself and His relationship with the Father and with believers.

I Am – the language of deity

In John 8:58, the Lord declared to the Jews that:

> "… before Abraham was, I am."

Their response was to try to stone Him because they recognised that He was taking upon Himself the language of deity. *Ego eimi* was used by God in the Old Testament to identify Himself. In Isaiah 40-55, which deals with Israel's glorious future deliverance by the work of the "suffering servant," God repeatedly describes Himself in these terms. For example:

> "Who has performed and done this, calling the generations from the beginning? I, the Lord, the first, and with the last; I am he" *(ego eimi)*. (Isaiah 41:4)

"I, I am he *(ego eimi)* who blots out your transgressions for my own sake, and I will not remember your sins." (Isaiah 43:25)

So, in John 8, Jesus was laying claim to that name and linking Himself with the God of the Old Testament. Elsewhere, Jesus stated this truth plainly, asserting that He and the Father are one (John 10:30) and that whoever had seen Him had seen the Father (John 14:9).

In other places in John's Gospel too, Jesus claimed *"ego eimi"* to dramatic effect. Perhaps the most striking example of this was in Gethsemane, when, confronted by armed soldiers, Jesus identified Himself to them by saying:

"I am he *(ego eimi)*". .. When Jesus said to them "I am he", they drew back and fell to the ground. (John 18:5-6)

This was an unusual response for armed soldiers, to say the least, and it suggests that they recognised that they were encountering someone who was much more than a village carpenter and itinerant teacher.

But in the seven well-known "I am" statements that we find in John's Gospel, the Lord taught His disciples a great deal more about His relationship with the Father and with them.

The Lord Jesus and the Father

Frequently, Jesus emphasised that He was sent by the Father, that His work was endorsed by the Father and that the Father's purpose of salvation was focused on Him. For example, in claiming to be the Bread of Life in John 6, He stated that the

Father had set His seal on Him (verse 27), that the Father had "given" Him to men and women (verse 32), that the work of God was to believe on the One the Father had sent (verse 29) and that the Father's will was that everyone who looks to the Son in faith should have eternal life (verse 40). In fact, Jesus came to do the will of the Father, rather than His own will (verse 38).

Not only so, but as the Good Shepherd, He had the Father's authority to lay down His life and to take it up again (John 10:18). Indeed, His willingness to go to the cross, in order to bring salvation to mankind was a reason that the Father loved Him (verse 17).

Yet, at the same time, the Lord did not just come as the Father's envoy, He came to reveal the Father and to demonstrate what the Father is like. Jesus taught the disciples about His oneness with the Father and to the Jews also He made a similar statement. In declaring Himself to be the Light of the world Jesus pointed out that, if they had known Him, they would have known the Father also (John 8:19).

However, perhaps the most important dimension of the Lord's work in this area is in bringing believers back into relationship with the Father. This is the over-riding aim of the Lord's work. No one comes to the Father except through Him, the Way, the Truth and the Life (John 14:6). He is *the* Door of the sheep, the only means of access to life (John 10:9-10). Anyone trying to enter by another way is a thief and a robber (John 10:1).

The Lord Jesus, then, stands between us and the Father, not to protect us from an angry God, but to bring the Father to us and to restore the relationship with the Father that was lost through our fallenness and sin.

But the "I AM" statements also reveal further truths about the Lord's relationship with believers.

The Lord Jesus and the believer

The Lord Jesus has restored our relationship with the Father, both for this life, and for eternity. He is the Resurrection and the Life and whoever believes in Him will never die (John 11:25-26). As the Light of the world He brings truth and life to mankind, revealing the Father to us and bringing us back to Him. In the opening chapter of his Gospel, John brings out the connection between light and life:

> In him was life, and the life was the light of men. (John 1:4)

The relationship into which we are brought is one of close personal knowledge. As the Good Shepherd He calls His sheep by name and leads them out. He goes before them and they follow Him because they know His voice (John 10:3-4). The Lord also protects His sheep – the Good Shepherd lays down His life for them (John 10:11). His protection is also evident in His role as the Door of the sheep, defending them from the "wolves, thieves and robbers" who might destroy the flock.

However, as we consider other metaphors we find that our relationship with the Lord Jesus is more intimate than sheep following a shepherd. We are not just followers of a great teacher and protector; our relationship is much closer. In His extended discourse in John 6, Jesus declared Himself to be the Bread of Life and invited His hearers to "eat" Him, in order to obtain eternal life.

"I am the living bread that came down from heaven. If anyone eats of this bread, he will live forever. And the bread that I will give for the life of the world is my flesh." (John 6:51)

This picture of "eating" the Bread of Life suggests that we will somehow take Him into ourselves and He will be part of who we are. In John 6, Jesus equates "eating" Him with "believing in Him." For example, we read:

"I am the bread of life: whoever comes to me shall not hunger and whoever believes in me shall never thirst." (verse 35)

"Truly, truly I say to you, whoever believes has eternal life… Whoever feeds on this bread will live forever." (verses 47, 58)

"Believing in Him" of course, is not merely mentally acknowledging certain truths, it involves committing ourselves to Him and obeying His commands. If we do that we will "abide" in him and He in us (John 6:56).

This idea of "abiding" in Him through obedience is explored in detail in Jesus' final picture of Himself as the True Vine, in John 15. There, our link with Him is so close and so dependent that we are pictured as branches of the vine that is Christ. The need to abide in Him is repeatedly affirmed. For example:

"Whoever abides in me and I in him, he it is that bears much fruit, for apart from me you can do nothing." (John 15:5)

This mutual abiding – us in Him and Him in us – is essential if we are to develop to Christian maturity. And the key to abiding is loving obedience:

> "If you keep my commandments you will abide in my love, just as I have kept my Father's commandments and abide in his love." (John 15:10)

We are called to a close personal relationship with Him, ministered through the Holy Spirit within us. But it is not simply a bilateral relationship between us and the Lord Jesus. It is important to recognise the activity and presence of the Father in the process of salvation.

The Lord Jesus, the Father and the believer

As we consider the *ego eimi* metaphors, we can see the hand of the Father at every stage. It is *the Father* who gives us the true bread from heaven (John 6:32) and no one can come to Jesus unless *the Father* draws him (John 6:44); when Jesus declared Himself to be the Light of the world, He called on the witness of *the Father*, who sent Him (John 8:16, 18); *the Father* loves Him and approved of His willingness to be the Good Shepherd, who laid down His life for His sheep (John 10:17); Jesus is the one and only true and living way to *the Father* (John 14:6); in the picture of the vine, we find *the Father* in the background, as the vinedresser (John 15:1), and the fruit borne by the branches is to the glory of *the Father* (John 15:8).

The wonderful truth contained in these pictures is that as Christian believers we are brought into relationship with the Lord Jesus *and* the Father, a relationship that will continue and will deepen, not only throughout our lives on this planet, but in eternity to come (John 17:3).

At the end of His discourse to the disciples in the upper room, the Lord prayed for them and for those who would subsequently come to faith through their ministry. In that prayer we can see something of the interconnectedness between the Lord Jesus, the Father and the believer and the unity that is central to it:

> "All mine are yours, and yours are mine, and I am glorified in them... (I ask) that they may all be one, just as you, Father, are in me, and I in you, that they also may be in us... I in them and you in me, that they may become perfectly one, so that the world may know that you sent me and have loved them even as you loved me." (John 17:10, 21, 23)

About the Author

W. M. Henry was born in Glasgow in 1949. He qualified as a Chartered Accountant and worked in the accountancy profession for a number of years before moving into academia. He is now retired and lives in Giffnock with his wife and two daughters.

Other publications by W M Henry, all of which are also available in print and as eBooks, include a major work on *The Trinity in John* (see next but one page for details) and the following titles:

The Signs in John's Gospel
No Condemnation (Romans 5:12-8:39)
Living in the Truth ... That you may know (1 John)
The Greatness of Christ ... The Speeches in Acts
By Faith Abraham ... The Making of a Man of God
Imitating Christ ... The Superiority of Christ (Hebrews)
Covenants: Old and New

He has also written two books with Michael Penny

Following Philippians
The Will of God: Past and Present

Both of these are available as perfect bound books and eBooks.

Further details of all the books mentioned on the following pages can be seen on

www.obt.org.uk

They can also be ordered from that website and also from:

The Open Bible Trust,
Fordland Mount, Upper Basildon,
Reading, RG8 8LU, UK.

They are also available as eBooks from Amazon and Apple and as KDP paperbacks from Amazon.

The Trinity in John

A Study in Relationships

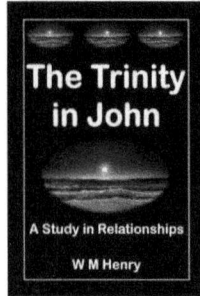

This book is a study of the relationships between the members of the Trinity and between the Trinity and Christian believers, focusing mainly on the Gospel of John.

The book opens with a discussion of the titles given to the Lord Jesus in John's Gospel and what they tell us about His relationship with His Father. The next two chapters explore the relationship between the Father and the Son and their joint work of redemption.

The book then widens the focus to examine the relationship between the Father, the Son and the believer before discussing the Holy Spirit and His relationship with other members of the Trinity, and with the believer.

Each chapter closes with brief meditative "Reflections" on the implications of the issues raised in the chapter. These are followed by suggestions for further study, which can be the basis for private devotions or group discussions.

Also by W M Henry

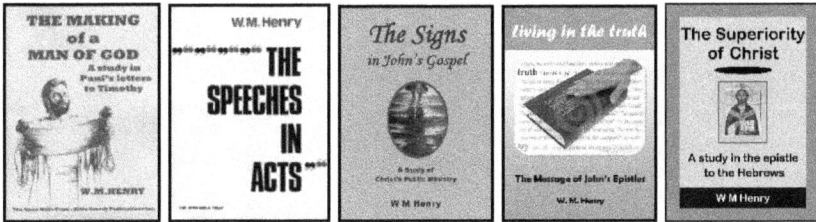

The Making of a Man of God
A study in Paul's letters to Timothy

The Speeches in Acts

The Signs in John's Gospel

Living in the truth
The Message of John's Epistles

The Superiority of Christ
A study in the epistle to the Hebrews

For further details of the above books, plus others written by
W M Henry, please visit:

www.obt.org.uk

Other works on John's Gospel

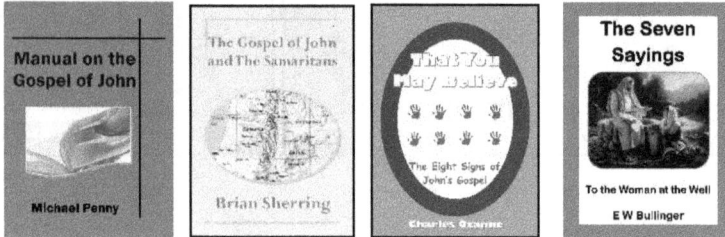

The Manual on the Gospel of John
By Michael Penny

John and the Samaritans
By Brian Sherring

That you may believe
The eight signs in John's Gospel
By Charles Ozanne

The Seven Sayings
To the Woman at the well
E W Bullinger

For further details of the above books, plus others on the Gospels, please visit:

www.obt.org.uk

About this book

The I AM
sayings of Jesus

One popular aspect of Jesus' teaching is His description of Himself using the formula "I am..."

Important lessons have been learned from studying the ways in which He is the light of the world, the good shepherd and so on. But what exactly did Jesus mean by the phrase "I am"?

The words in Greek are *ego eimi* and when we examine the way Jesus uses this phrase, we discover that He is doing much more than making descriptive statements about Himself.

These book explores how Jesus uses the expression *ego eimi* in John's Gospel and considers something of what it means.

Publications of The Open Bible Trust must be in accordance with its evangelical, fundamental and dispensational basis. However, beyond this minimum, writers are free to express whatever beliefs they may have as their own understanding, provided that the aim in so doing is to further the object of The Open Bible Trust. A copy of the doctrinal basis is available on **www.obt.org.uk** or from:

THE OPEN BIBLE TRUST
Fordland Mount, Upper Basildon,
Reading, RG8 8LU, UK